NOIRMALE

MISCONCEPTIONS OF A LOST MAN

Chief Yuya T. Assaan-ANU
Anu Publishing
www.ChiefYuya.com

HRU Yuya T. Assaan-ANU / Chief Yuya

Table of Contents

Livication 5

Preface 7

Normal 15

Tin Man 25

NoirMale 31

Beauty-N-The-Beast 39

HRU 47

Drowning 55

Thin Line 61

Conclusion 69

NoirMale Music 73

About the Author 75

LIVICATION

This work is for every male who finds himself drowning in a sea of unreasonable expectations, disappointments, anger, directionless, depression, regret, identity confusion, despair, hope, struggle, and personal validation.

May my Sun's never know the pain of crawling through the world without a ray of direction or sense of belonging. I will labor , without end, to keep it that way.

To all of the young men who view me as a Father figure. Then that I am. Let us build!

To my creators and makers: Abu Jeremiah, Baba Gil, Uncle James, and most importantly Grandfather R. Lee and Grandfather C. Stinson there are too many gems and gifts to thank you for so, I will simply say, I honor you. You have given a great legacy to aspire to. Asante Sana!

PREFACE

I would like you to gain a greater command of the emotional and mental framework of men. Most importantly, the melanin rich man is the subject of this determined undertaking. You will hear me use the terms "melanin rich", "melanin dominant", "Black", "Negro", "Moor" and "Original" interchangeably throughout this manuscript.

Theoretically, I would like to assign this prelude to The Central Park 5 for demonstrative perspective. This horrifying saga is a prime example of the injustice waged against the Negro male in American society. In this ghastly ordeal we find one of the most blatant illustrations, in recent history, of the demonization of the melanin rich male.

The Central Park 5

On April 19, 1989 Trisha Meili was physically assaulted and raped in Central Park. This 843-acre park is a well-known gathering place where people go to exercise, picnic, and enjoy group activities in New York City. At the same time Trisha Meili was being attacked, allegedly, there were a group of about 20-30 young people in another vicinity who were aimlessly attacking people in the same park.

Reportedly, several other joggers and bicyclist were assaulted and robbed in this park around the time of the attack and rape of this female jogger. Apparently, the attack on this 28-year-old jogger was so severe that she suffered head trauma causing her to go into a 12-day coma and, permanently, lose memory of the events of that night. Although her condition was originally considered to be terminal, as she was given her final rites while in coma, she recovered and by the grace of heaven was able to jog again just 3-4 months after the happening.

Regrettably, there were six young males who were incriminated and detained for the rape and attempted murder of Trisha Meili. These young men were Steve Lopez, 14, Antron McCray, 15, Kevin Richardson, 14, Yusef Salaam, 15, Raymond Santana, 14, and Korey Wise, 16. All young men were initially interrogated without the presence of a guardian or legal representation. Despite being coerced into false confessions by way of physical abuse, threats, and mind games they were indicted on charges of rape, sodomy, attempted murder, and rioting. In less than 30 days they all had recanted the coerced confessions citing that they made them under threat of their lives. This made no difference. In 1991, Steve Lopez entered into a plea agreement for an attack on another citizen and had never acknowledged any participation in the attack on Trisha Meili. As a result, he was sentenced to 1.5 to 4.5 years in a juvenile facility for the mugging of jogger John Loughlin. He was removed from the case involving Trish Meili. Consequently, we have the "Central Park 5" which is comprised of the remaining young boys. On April 26, 1989 The New York Times printed an article entitled "**The Jogger and the Wolf Pack**". This rarely mentioned article was only a forerunner to what was to come next.

On May 1, 1989 Donald Trump took out an $85,000 full-page advertisement in the New York Times entitled, "**Bring Back the Death Penalty. Bring Back out Police**". In this article he called for the death of these young men. On May 10th the Central Park 5 were indicted. The first trial of Antron McCray, Yusef Salaam, and Raymond Santana did not begin until June 25th, of 1990.

Many of you reading this may know that the Central Park 5 were found guilty of the charges levied against them despite forced confession, a lack of evidence, conflicting confessions, and huge gaps in logic and procedure of the case. The four youngest defendants served between 6-7 years, individually. Korey Wise served 13 years (he was tried as an adult because of his 16 years of age), up until a confession from the actual perpetrator of the crime, Matias Reyes, came forth. He confessed, in 2001, while serving a life sentence for rape and murder. At the time he was incarcerated with Korey Wise and saw the violent handling Wise had received throughout the years and had a moment of moderation and came forth to tell what he had actually committed. He was never tried for the crime because, by that time, the atrocity that he acted out had passed the legal statute of limitations.

Incongruously, shortly after this incident that occurred with Trisha Meili there was another attack on a black woman in the borough of Brooklyn. On May 3, 1989, allegedly, a 30-year-old black woman was raped, robbed, and then thrown from the roof of a building, falling 50 feet. No full-page ads were taken out for the woman attacked in Brooklyn. Fortunately, she survived even after having to endure extensive rehabilitation and hospitalization. There were three young men indicted in the case. Tyrone Prescott, 17, Kelvin Furman, 22, and Darron Decoteau, 17, were arrested and eventually took plea deals for the incident. Prescott and Furman were sentenced to 6 to 18 years in prison, while Decoteau was sentenced to 4-12 years. This particular incident received little to no media notice. This legal event highlighted the difference in prosecution and media coverage between a white victim and a black one.

After all charges against the Central Park 5 were vacated on December 19, 2002, they pursued legal action against the state and city of New York. Prior to the clearing of these charges these alleged defendants not only had to register themselves on the New York State sex offender registry but, had to suffer the indignities of not being able to find employment or housing because of prior convictions. In the midst of this legal action there were portions of the community, as well as their defense attorneys, who stated that Donald Trump owed these, now, full grown men an apology. Below I provide just a small sample of President Donald Trump's response:

- **"You have people on both sides of that."**
- **"They admitted their guilt."**
- **"Settling doesn't mean innocent."**
- **"These young men do not exactly have the pasts of angels."**

When the individuals who were falsely accused and imprisoned were awarded a $41 million settlement Donald Trump stated:

- **"It's a disgrace".**
- **"The police doing the original investigation say they were guilt. The fact that that case was settled with so much evidence against them is outrageous. And the woman , so badly injured, will never be the same."**
- **"Innocent of what-how many people did they mug?"**

Consider the $85,000 in 1989 ($182,000 in 2020 based on the rate of inflation) that Trump spent on his full-page New York Times advertisement that stated, 'now was a time not to analyze but, to hate'. Donald Trump has not retracted one statement but, has made sure to reaffirm all of his previous assertions. The innocence of these men has been disputed by the original NYC police detectives involved with the case, commentator Ann Coulter, and the original prosecuting legal team.

I highlight President Trump's statements, then and now, because his sentiment typifies the historical opinion the world has had of Negro people, in general. President Trump, is arguably, one of the most powerful men in the world. The attitude that he carries is one that is disseminated to his constituents. The agenda laced outlook that president Trump operates from is not a new one. He is upholding a long-standing legacy of tyranny and racism, upon which the sub-corporation known as the "United States of America" was built upon.

In order to further protect the survival of his own genetics the emerging Caucasian male found it necessary to establish, as wide a wedge as possible between his family and the Negroid one. The Black male and female had to be consciously reduced to the sentimentality held for "beast of the field" if they were to be controlled, utilized, and kept away from the slave master's gene pool. This campaign against Negro masculinity is nothing short of a militaristic undertaking. As we see in the monetary investment that Mr. Trump was able to put forth to rally the temperament of his comrades, there is nothing that the adversary will not do to cement the sub-human perception of the Negro male and female into the minds of all those who would lend an ear.

This work will urge us to ask the following question:

"Why is it so easy to vilify the negro male, and what has that historical PSYOP done to him?".

NORMAL

1

This work is primarily directed towards the struggles males go through in endeavoring to achieve a state of normalcy while rectifying that standard of normality with their own biological inborn sense of rightness. The inner conflict between what is dictated and what is innate can be the fine line between enslavement and freedom. Men are natural born explorers and, in that, must be free to rove. The first exploration is an excursion into the multi-sensory experience that the immediate environment offers up. The reaction to the ecosystem begins to sculpt what one's worldview is, even in infancy. Babies love to put objects in their mouths. Frankly, that habit hardly ceases into adulthood. The sense of taste and touch takes on an enormous role in identifying what is pleasing or disagreeable within a child's immediate surroundings. The disciplining that they receive from their guardian figures begins the division between right or wrong for them, despite what their wits reveal to them.

In Western society, rightness is dictated. Habitually, a code of conduct is imported by way of religion and early schooling. The purpose of a religion is to install a program which will calibrate the adherent to the design and purpose of that religion. Schooling is provided to increase the productivity and skill relevancy of the attendees.

The question of normalcy raises so many sequential queries depending on personal history and social surroundings. As individuals endeavor to achieve normalcy, they frequently wind up cannibalizing their sense of naturalness. Sadly, in current times we are suffering a fine disparity between what is normal and what is natural. In fact, natural is often suppressed in lieu of normalcy. Normal functions within a civilization that defines what normal is, and what normal does. The million-dollar question is, who governs the society that creates that standard and description for normal?

Culture defines our canons and worldview. As we travel through the hyper-stimulated setting, we call society, do we ever take time out to determine what culture we are living? Culture is a tool that is utilized to establish and reinforce what is normal. Within our culture we will receive our language, music, religion, sexual practices, eating habits, politics, and so on. When we can conform ourselves to the standards unstated or overtly taught that align with those various components of culture, then we can realize a state of social normalcy.

Social normality is not an aspiration strictly reserved for sheep-like people. There is nothing wrong with wanting or striving to claim the understanding and criteria of what the leaders of your community outline to you. The problem we run into is when we are in a situation, wherein we do not have a lineage connection to the leaders of our communities. When the spearheads of our communities are, in fact, utilizing us for their own personal interests. Then their conferred sense of normalcy will be a standard based around usury and manipulation. There are many aspects of western culture that we find ourselves engrossed in without any real explanation of the base motivation of those practices. We see some of the most genius minds create rebellion inside of elementary schools by asking the question, "why do we have to do this"?

"Why" is a great question but, should be preceded by the proper enquiry of "What?". It is important that we research *"what"* is normal before we even look at *"why"* is normal. In fact, we must look at *"what, how, and why"*.

- What do we consider to be normal?
- How is normalcy achieved?
- Why is the standard for normalcy what it is?

What is Normal?

There is no absolute when it comes to normalization. Normalizing is based on a desired barometer. That bar is determined by the ability to display requirements for an aptitude to complete a specific function. In public school settings this is called "standardization". Government standards inaugurate the tone for public standards. There is great anxiety surrounding the achieving of government standards. Young people are indoctrinated with those encryptions for seven hours per day inside of school bodies. Of course, *actual education* would interfere with the process of standardizing.

Through the forceful imputing of a standard of normal, we lose our identities at an early age. There is no commendation towards the great pursuits in life imparted in the basic classes held in learning facilities. In schools we are taught how to obey the daily subservience expected from the authoritative powers that be. This is not a condemnation towards the educators that function inside of those schools. Many of them are kindhearted, caring, and devoted. Unfortunately, the learning facilities are culturally psychopathic and the proxies that work within them are misinformed.

We must take a deeper look at the standard of regulation we flock to. We are being normalized based upon function. If we are not determining what our purpose is on the planet, then our standards for normalization will only be purposeful for another. We are often cited as abnormal based on the actions we perform that people observe. We are considered normal, or abnormal, based on what we display. What we "are" does not matter as long as we will perform the work of those who define what our functions are. These classifications are imparted by culture and most often, for younger people, school and media.

How are we Normalized?

As mentioned above, our socialization begins at a very young age. By the time we receive our name and are fed a recommended diet, the process is already in full swing. Culture is the imparted conception of our place in the universe that begins the sculpting of what we see as being normal for what we are. In most instances this begins with the fairytales and myths that have been shared with us. Those fairytales and myths may be allegorical and religious-based or serve to install cultural patterns. In Western cultural it is fair to deduce that the reigning aristocrats would rather their subjects be uninformed and compliant based upon the labyrinth of red tape and secret documents one needs to unearth simply to learn what should be the plainest of legislative objective. In order to create a populace such as this, the collective dumbing down must begin right at the age that a child's curiosity which allows them to formulate the question "Why?".

When young boys are told stories such as "Hansel and Gretel", "Goldie Locks and the Three Bears", "Little Red Riding Hood", "Sleeping Beauty", and "Snow White and the 7 Dwarfs" they are being taught to suspend their disbelief. There are questions that arise that they are told to suppress in order to enjoy what is being presented. A small sample of these rudimentary questions could be:

- "What kind of parents would allow two small children to go wandering off into the woods?"
- "Wouldn't a house made of candy be unhygienic, or melt?"
- "Why was it OK for a small girl to break and enter into the home of three bears?"
- "Since when do bears live in houses and eat porridge?"
- "How could a young girl not be able to recognize her grandmother from a wolf? Was she blind?"
- "How could a mirror, which is inanimate, tell someone who the "fairest" of them all is, considering a mirror does not even live int he real world but, reflects only a two-dimensional image?"
- "How is it that eating your stepdaughters' lungs and liver will make you as beautiful as she is?"
- "Is cannibalism normal?"

These questions only scratch the surface as we still have cartoons, music, and film to address in the normalization of the young child.

To collectively enjoy these ideas with their peers, young people are coerced into accepting the unacceptable. They must abandon reason and suspend their disbelief of nonsensical notions. If they choose to insist upon further investigation of the non-mathematical chants, myths, religious archetypes, and imparted rules they are labeled as uncooperative and rebellious. The more the child complies with the concepts that are disharmonious within their own natural born instinct and intelligence, they begin to develop a cognitive dissonance. This does not fade, but rather they learn to live with it. The value of free thought is degraded and devalued before the age of seven.

There is nothing inherently wrong with myth, folklore, or the study of heavenly bodies. In fact, these are all healthy constituents of sentient culture. The trouble arises when these stories are presented in a way that does not instigate discussions around the metacognition and mental alchemy that all children are capable of. These stories provide information about the archetypical influences that exist inside of the human psyche. When young people are taught about the separation between the egotistical self and the true spiritual self, they can watch these stories and see the symbolism of what ideas and concepts they are being advised to sustain. The insertion of talking animals with human-like consciousness in all of these myths should provide an understanding of the hierarchy of development that young people are expected to ascend, from animal-like to god-like.

Why are we Normalized?

For society to advance forward there must be a categorizing and organizing of gears that would uniformly work together. This means that individuals within a society must be classified based on their ability and pre-determinations. When this is done effectively, the social structure is able to advance forward with its intended idea and agenda. Of course, this may not always work in the best interest for those who would like to experience a native-born pitch of autonomy. When you have those who choose to do what their free wits dictate, despite the propositioning from the larger social environment, they are usually considered to be anomalies. These people are given titles such as rebel, stubborn, abnormal, oddballs, and so forth.

To create normality is to fulfill someone's vision. Who would determine what normal is other than the person who conjures a pre-cognition of what another individual is supposed to be? In essence, your normalizer is your maker. Often, I find myself internally correcting a well-known term before it exits my lips. That phrase is "slave master". I repeatedly have to remind myself that there are no *slave masters* but only slave *makers*. For there to be a slave master, someone must have been a slave first in need of mastery. In truth, people who are converted into slaves were firstly free people. The people who convert them are their makers. This is not to be confused with their *Creator*.

So, why are people normalized? People are normalized so they can fulfill the vision of someone who existed before them. People are controlled so that they can consummate the function of someone who seeks to progress a concept forward into full manifestation. This could be your parents, teachers, Family Elders, mate, boyfriend/girlfriend, internal parasite or even your own offspring. Whomever harbors expectations for another, could potentially seek to standardize the other person based on the grid lines of those expectations. Those anticipations may be for their own personal gain or they may be based around something that they would like to see for that person. Nonetheless, whether a person has a pure agenda or one that is fastened with nefarious motives, to have anyone seek to form you based on their ceiling of awareness of what normal is, could never be a godlike venture.

Many global ruling bodies seek a large portion of control over its population. For instance, when the United States declared bankruptcy in the 1930's, there was a need to utilize the citizens of the country as collateral for the governmental debt. How could you establish this way of being as a norm without a civil uprising? The culture that is deposited into the minds of citizens becomes the regulator for that long arm reach of control. As mentioned previously, once a child is taught to live with their cognitive dissonance, they will passively learn to live with laws that make no sense and do not serve what should be their inalienable rights. This makes it much easy to impose rule over human beings.

TIN MAN

2

The strength of manhood can be made allegorical to steel, as in "the man of steel". This does not mean that the man has no soft vulnerable underbelly. The trials of his life require him to become stoic and hardened. There is always a moment in which that, seemingly impenetrable, man must trust someone to perform the needed maintenance on his metallic physique.

There is a deliberate misconception perpetuated about men which states that they have little access to their feelings, other than those that encourage violence. This is a weaponized fallacy. In a society where terms like "Man up!" are constantly chanted into the ears of young males seeking to cope with their own disappointments, the notion of suppressing the entirety of the ground swell of their feelings becomes a perverse mark of maturity among young males.

Indeed men must know how to temporarily suppress their feelings and productively channel their emotions more than any genus because, in the lead position, they are required to continually navigate with clarity. Men are not *allowed* to "freak out" or breakdown from stress related ordeals. If a man, for any reason, steps away from the controls of the proverbial plane he is flying, he and the entire crew (family and community) are subject to crash and burn. The importance of the idea of *temporary suppression* can not be overstated. Unfortunately, there are times when individuals will capitalize on the male's necessary skill of focus in the time of turmoil and misrepresent this as callousness. If the developing male hears this bogus claim long enough he begins to believe that stone-heartedness is an expected characteristic of masculinity.

This emotional pressure causes many males to withhold their true feelings for their loved ones as their expressions are often overlooked or misunderstood. At a time when superfluous outpourings of affection and adoration are poured into the ears of unguarded females, a standard of emotional expression is established that works against the natural inclinations of men. There is a defined line that exist between the male and female genus. In a society that seeks to control both parties, the blurring of those lines has proven to be most effective.

When there are demands placed upon women to communicate with the emotional suppression and clarity of men they begin to lost group on the ordering of their own mental spaces. When a man is told that his emotions are his point of weakness and despite the trauma he faces, there should be no post traumatic condition to speak about aloud or contend with. Typically men are told that any personal ailment can be resolved with the upturning of a bottle of alcohol, a handful of narcotics, or a rowdy night of attachment free sex. When the male expresses to his natural mate that all he desires is her time and her ability to cool the embers of his day with her cool watery mystique, it is commonly overlooked.

The emotional investments of a man are very precious to him. Many marital rifts are caused because he feels unsupported and under-appreciated. When a woman is excited about what a man is invested in, he becomes deeply endeared to her. In a highly competitive world, men have to hide their aspirations and dreams as it would prove to be of great detriment to their agenda to let the world know what they are thinking. To have one person that he can share his moments of joy and pain with are what many yearn for.

The woman is the natural complement of the man. She mirrors his nature, with her own. When you are interacting with the individual that the Creator of all has mated you with, there is no need to hide feelings and thoughts. The term "mate" means "match". A mate is your match, which can also be seen as your complement as we know that the male and female design are not identical but, they naturally connect. We can observe in the anatomical form of the male and female that event their most vulnerable parts "fit" together. To consider that the logical expression cradles perfectly into the emotional womb of the woman. In fact, it is logic and thought that stimulates energy to motion. In this, we see emotion is energy or electricity in motion. As the woman can express her emotions and find ordering in the consciousness of the man, it is the man who can witness the observance of his mental energy in active motion by the emotional reaction of his feminine counterpart.

When a thought of stress or worry is expressed, even latently there should be an emotional response. A true man does not need logical, or rational ordering from his mate. When a man ask, "What would I do with out you?", he is expressing one of the paramount ideas within the context of his mission. A man wielding this sort of query is expression ing that the female, in context, is vital to his inner workings and achievements. The female who is able to assist the male in achieving his goals becomes his modeling for his divinely intended help meet. Often that assistances comes by way of her emotional reactions to his mental offerings. She transfers her emotions of excitement, confidence, awe, and general positivity back into the man. When she is indifferent, he becomes despondent he slowly loses the purpose and meaning in his work.

The heart mind connection is vital in us all but, in mating to be able to send the energy of the male heart into the female mind, and subsequently the female heart into the male mind is crucial in establishing healthy bond pairing between the two. A bona-fide male ask for little more than genuine connection but, this can not be forced. There is a true chemistry that must be inherent in the linkage.

NOIRMALE

3

The double entendre "Noirmale" is the founding rudiment of this entire literary mission. When we hear the term "Noir", most often we are being directed towards an artistic genre surrounding a lack of moralism and filled with cynicism. "Film Noir" is a genre of film that generally portrays depression, fatalism, and frequently a spirit of menace through the use of certain sound elements, film filters, and pessimistic writing style. It was in the 1940's that this style of filming was popularized as a response to the upbeat and cheerful propaganda films of the 1930's that were designed to relieve the depression of Word War II and the economic collapse known as "The Great Depression".

The word noir is a french one meaning "black". When applied to art or film it is usually termed as "dark" because of the intended mood but, the phrase *Film Noir*, literally means Black Film. This style of film almost always revolves around a criminal element. Usually these stories are lead by a private investigator, morally corrupt cop, hopeless athlete, or someone who has recently become corrupted due to a series of events. The Noir genre of film usually depicts events of cruelty and will show and stylings with influence

—

from the German Expressionism movement of the 1920's. It should be noted that this style of artistic expression is a bit ambiguous in that the elements present in what would be "Noir" could be found in many other style of films.

Noir is a derisive of the word "Niger", which later became Negro. In the mid 1500's this term Negro was utilized to classify the "black-skinned" race of Arica". Prior to that a common term was Aethiops, which today we know as Ethiopian.

I mention the genre of "Noir" for reasons that help us to understand the undertaking of social engineering. Since the 1940's we have been offered this term "Noir" as an allusion to something morally reprehensible and sleazy. In these films the protagonist is usually also someone who is saturated with a criminal element, or is a criminal. So, with that we are focused on "the bad guy". Consider motion pictures such as "Dracula". The early renditions of this story would be considered Noir style The same can be said for films like "The Mummy", which was realized in 1932. Ironically, it is no secret that many of the indigenous cultures of the African continent venerate ancestral spirits. To make a film that depicts an Egyptian ancestor as a villain, is a clear sign of a larger agenda to demonize, and criminalize, the idea of "Negro" and Africa. When we fast forward we see films such as Soylent Green (1973), Taxi Driver (1976), Blade Runner (1982), Basic instinct (1992), The Matrix (1999), Training Day

(2001), Insomnia (2002) and Sin City (2005), and Thirst (2009) all presenting the noir style of film.

When we look at the word "male", of course, there is a reference to masculinity. Interesting enough, when you observe classical definition of the word male, there is a reference to the sex which "begets", in contrast to the feminine which is considered the sex which conceives and births. To beget something simply means to attain a particular thing by the employment of effort. So, we see there is a proactive nature present in the idea of begetting. The prefix "be" means to come into existence or to represent a happening of some sort, similar to the biblical statement "I am". "I am" is an ultimate statement of being. If you were to *go get* something, you would have to go and acquire that thing. The concept of "getting" something is not a difficult one. Loosely stated, often, when coitus is mentioned there is a reference of "getting some". So, the male has always had the defining onus of getting placed upon him. This is why we would consider the masculine principle to be the one which is the proactive one because it reaches out to attain and seize something. In the early 14th center the term "get" was used to classify a child. If you go to certain parts of the world, up until this day, you will still hear the term "get/git" used to refer to a small child.

With our literal definitions outlined for Noirmale, we must explore the phonetics of the term. NoirMale has a word sound similar to "Normal", this is purposefully and artfully done.

- Is NoirMale normal?
- Is Normal Black Male?
- Is NoirMale Immoral Male?

These are the questions that are the pivot point of this entire discussion that you and I are having. As we are fight for our own natural sense of normalcy we find ourselves fighting an uphill battle against social definitions that have already criminalized us from the moment of our begetting and conception. There has been an outcry dating back from the burgeoning of the civil rights moment in, North America, which centered around Negro people struggling to change the perception that their oppressors and slave makers held for them. In recent times there has been the "Black Lives Matter" movement. These are both attempts to appeal to the consciousness of individuals and groups who may hold an ideation about dark skinned races from Africa that is less than benevolent and certainly not one of equability.

"To the real question, How does it feel to be a problem?
I answer seldom a word."
- W.E.B. DuBuois ***"The Souls of Black Folk"***

In this monumental work the great pro activist and writer, W.E.B. DuBuois, states that there is an ever present underlying hatred towards the Negro race. Imagine waking up everyday and knowing that you are an unsolved problem for an entire group of people differentiated from your own by racial designation. With all of the challenges that exist such as the accumulation of wealth, proper education, developing a spiritual life, establishing fine homes there is the additional bane of the Negro problem. This creates a duality of mindset within the melanin-rich individual. The more they achieve, the more they remind those who find them to be a peculiar sort of problem are reminded of them.

The challenges of integration are infested with the "Negro problem". There is a valorizing of "Whiteness" that becomes the standard for Negro achievement. The melanin rich race's aspiration to integrate is based around the notion that the lifestyles, and associated privileges non-blacks enjoy represent the normalized standard for human existence. The "white standard" now becomes the new normal for the dark skin African living under the yolk of White society. For the Negro man, this becomes a more more radicalized problem when his natural propensity tells him there is a standard more fitting for him but, those within his own household, in particular his mate, are determined to hold him to a White standard of normalcy.

From the failed attempts of trying to acclimate one into a form that psychically, biologically, spiritually, and culturally do no speak to the identify of the Negro, we then witness a swift descent into lunacy. So much of this angst is a product of the integration politics that fuel the integration problem.

By promoting the idea of the White standard as normal, the inevitable result is the vilifying of the Negro standard. The "problem" becomes the actual natural state of the Negro. The assumptive normative of Whiteness creates a stigma towards anything that cultivates "Blackness". The problem continues despite efforts to integrate because of the growing lunacy within the aspiring integrating Negro. Who would be happy about having a lunatic integrate within their ranks? If Blackness, or even poverty, becomes stigmatized with a criminal undertone how would those non-blacks living beyond such strife ever accept those who are indelibly marked with blackness into their society? In fact, the very *ambition* of the Negro becomes a problem. The Whites normalize their standard of living as the standard and proclaim that is people should aspire to but, when non-whites close in on that established bar they, instantly, represent a grave problem.

The solution lies in the Negro's ability to establish a functional standard that establishes an identity based on his, or her, self determining drive. Inside of a family, there is a circulatory validation that moves throughout the unit. We receive our first commendations of self verification inside of our families. When the form of those natural forming families is weakened by a side assault of alien culture, the foundations of validation become breached and rendered ineffective. The strength of the family leads the charge for

the heart and character of the self defining cast of normal for
the Black Male.

———

BEAUTY-N-THE-BEAST

4

"Beauty lies deep within my carbon"

There is a great distinction between what is gorgeous and what is beautiful. Beauty is a phenomenon that can only be observed at the parallel of the soul because it is a perceived reflection from the soul. Beauty is the effect of an authentic connection with an upper benign power. To perceive something, we must possess that same thing we are distinguishing. Beauty, similar to healing, is an energy that emanates from the interior and then moves to the exterior. What we see exhibited on the outer shell is a product of what resides inside that encasement. Therefore, we must perceive things that are internal by using our inner eye.

To be gorgeous, attractive, dazzling, pleasing, lovely, sexy, handsome, pretty, comely, and the like are typically only surface manifestations of intended core presence. Most importantly, these superficial displays are culturally relative, as opposed to beauty which is universally perceived by those with the ability to identify it. So often we are mesmerized by the manipulation of our sense of touch, smell, sight, hearing, and taste. When we lost our ability to differentiate what lies beneath the sensation of our carnal senses, we begin to imagine all that exist is what we can tangibly process. This is when the tragedy of great suffering begins to enter into our lives.

Men must implement an outlook of austerity into their lives in order to keep from being deterred by, the dazzling shows of somatic temptations that exist throughout the biosphere. It is the pining and craving for material substances that induce suffering. The material grid provides satisfaction for our carnality but, the greater mission lies in a timely discovery that the sensual body is never really satisfied. The unceasing hunt for this bottomless pit of satisfaction becomes the suffering that many experience in the form of addictions and depression. Suffering is a product of the mental attachments we sustain around all things earthly, **whether they be relationships, possessions, or aspirations.**

Is it possible we become beautiful by acts and gorgeous by, "chance"?

In Western society the Negro male is depicted as a harsh, oversexed, ravenous, violent, stalwart brute. This is reinforced in numerous subliminal advertising campaigns, film, and music. Films such as DW Griffith's 1915 drama, "The Birth of a Nation" displays the newly liberated African Moor man as a brutal rapist with an obsession for Caucasian women. The film suggests the potential dangers of racial integration in the antebellum south while portraying the Klu

Klux Klan as the valiant knights emerging to restore balance and dispense justice. The ideas represented in this film are still preserved until this day throughout many inventive works.   Films/Books like *Red Rock* (1898), *The Clansman* (1905), *Tarzan* (1912), *The Littlest Rebel* (1935), *How Sleeps the Beast* (1937), *Gone with the Wind* (1939), *Fantasia* (1940), *Dumbo* (1941), *Song of The South* (1946), *Luther* (1952), *The Sin Smugglers* (1963), Planet of the Apes (1968), *Mandingo* (1975), *Drum* (1976), *The Color Purple* (1982), *The Toy* (1982), *Soul Man* (1986), *Glory* (1989), *What's love got to do with it* (1993), *Nothing to Lose* (1997), *Rush Hour* (1998), *Star Wars: Episode I - The Phantom Menace* (1999), *Training Day* (2001), *Bringing Down the House* (2003), *Precious* (2009), and more all labor to thoroughly reinforce the image and idea of the black male beast and his never ending pursuit to ravage what is most precious to his white male counterpart, the white woman. These projects also provide the portrayal of dim witted, servile, uncouth, animal-like, non-thinking Negro men and women. All of these works construct a Black Male identity that has very little to do with the genuine in-born character of black males, or men for that matter.

While encoding of this magnitude exists along such a long timeline, and is still actively propagated, it becomes very difficult for one to articulate an image of Negro masculinity that speaks to the beautiful nature of the masculine realization of the planet's first people. Racist films, music, books, and the like persistently represent the black male as someone who we all must be protected from, even his own wife and children are not safe from his mistreatment and incompetence. He is forever the quick tempered, alcoholic, oblivious, violent, scheming, cheating, sexually perverse, immature, unskilled, godless cretin the family must tolerate or escape from. Hollywood provides the *blameless* black woman or white woman as the virtuous victim of the black male and all of his *demonic wiles*. This identity has become the inescapable iron mask bolted onto the necks of Negro men in the Anglosphere. The crusade towards self-definition and cultural reclamation has already been anticipated and there are caricatures that await the melanin-rich man along that passageway. When the personal awakening of the dark skin African stimulates a movement towards mental freedom and the breaking of the bonds of stereotyping, there is a substitute typecast that awaits the individual. This displays ones of the most diabolical games of human chess.

If the Negro man reacts heatedly to the incursion on his livelihood, home, family, body, spirituality, God, or culture he is stigmatized with the "Angry Black Male" identity. If he chooses to immerse himself in intellectual purity to understand the psychological, emotional, economical, and kinship ramifications of his historical oppression and neocolonialism, then he is ridiculed for being a "Hotep" or "one of those pro-blacks". Whichever way he turns to free himself of the shackles of a manufactured boorish identity, he will have to endure ridicule from those he most treasures. This takes a colossal amount of mettle and is a great feat, within itself. The consciously black male receives no incentives for fighting his way towards a liberated body and free mind. In the process he will lose spouses, children, finances, employment, reputation, and more. Many original men do not know this truth before they begin their passage but, soon discover it. This crossing may further cement the image of him as a hardened beast, as war tends to do, but it positively cultivates the nature of beauty within him.

Deception is what fuels the spirit of girlish unaccountability that so many men find themselves prey to in Western society. As we have read above, the dark-skinned African male has been demonized for the purposes of control and social distancing. The dark-skinned African female has been infantilized and elevated for the purpose of being an in-house agent for the controlling procedure of the Negro male. We see this demonstrated in the 1977 movie "Roots". It is the character William Reynolds, who states "Mammy Belle is as true and loyal a woman as the Almighty ever let draw breath" in reference to his female house slave. This statement was said before he sold Belle's daughter, Kizzy, to another plantation owner who then raped and impregnated the young teenager with her only child. In truth, neither male nor female are truly winning.

Negro females in the western world are taught to acclaim everything about themselves which hinders the sustaining of a wholesome household. She is told to mask the natural beauty that her Creator has bestowed upon her and strive for an aesthetic that she will never be able to achieve. Her standard of normal is manipulated by her inner struggle with vanity. In the Anglosphere the dark skin African female is used as the agent of destruction within the melanin rich homestead. This is not her natural intention or standing but, she has been trained to become this contract instrument inside of the melanin-dominant people. It is the female who teaches the progeny of a community. There is no ruler who has ever ruled a nation who was not first been ruled over, and prepared for adulthood, by his mother. There are individuals, who have spent an exuberant about of time studying the lives of African people, who are aware that the way to the resources of the melanin dominant populace is through the manipulation of the dark skin African female's mind. If a wedge can be driven between the natural assembly between the original male and the original female, the line of communication between them can be detoured. As a result of this intrusion, a "new" man can emerge as the guiding light and navigator for the dark skin African female. Natural disruption is the basis of the "Willie Lynch" enslavement process concept. If the melanin dominant man chooses to rebel against this reliance procedure he is immediately classified as unruly, uncooperative, destructive, violent, and a hinderance to the progress of the family (which now becomes only the female and the children she has birthed for the man).

The dark skin female is always represented by the "Beauty" and her male counterpart as "The Beast". However, is there beauty in the beast or is the beauty really the beast?

When we look at the heinous process that has been calculated and effected for the children of the enslaved in North America, it is no wonder that the organic process of conjoining and establishing family has become such a perilous course. There is a wedge that has been driven between the two and the love that was once celebrated through song, dance, and poetry has been militarized. Sadly, there are times where one side of the gender equation actually feels as though they have the upper hand over the other because of the "game" or moves that they have been trained to use on one another. These competitions do not conclude with the formation of stable families, communities, or the reversal of the seasoning process that began when their ancestors were first loaded into, the hulls of trade ships. I repeat my previous statement: *Neither male nor female are truly winning.*

HRU

5

The concept of the "hero" is an age-old motif and many interpretive examples can be found in ancient religions and world mythology. The typical hero treatment involves some sort of extraordinary birth, a series of trials that the hero undergoes in their youth, the pursuit of a quest, and then a reward at the end of their heroic feats and trials. Throughout this progression there is a constant proving of the nature and birthright of said protagonist, even if they are the "unlikely hero" archetype. What I describe here represents a typical pattern but, there are variations. For example, in Greek mythos we often see the hero living a life of misery or dying what is called a "hero's death" at the end of their journey. The reward for overcoming the trials throughout their quest is not always a life of fulfillment but, rather a decent into the kingdom of hades.

The life of the Negro Male, globally, has been a non-stop replay of the latter pattern of the hero's life. The unusual birth is the loveless illegitimate couplings so many are conceived under while living on economic plantations and societal reservations. The early test is the obstacle course of control perpetuated by lower institutions of training called public schools. The quest is the pursuit for a genuine definition of manhood amidst all of the pervasive peripheral authority that would tell the young man what his deliberation of his specialness ought to be. After the conclusion of this mission he finds that the more he knows, the more miserable his daily existence becomes because of his newly expanded vision and sensitivity to the poisons he finds himself walled by.

The concept of hero worship is a fairly recent one when we look at the anthropological timeline. We see cults of hero worship in classical Greece used as a means to provide homage to individuals who died, or lived, in a way that was considered significant. Often this worship was performed at gravesites wherein the individuals buried were not even known to the venerators. The celebrants would fabricate a personality for the "dead", *which is one of the original transliterations of the word "hero"*, in order to **create** an impression of great times gone by and the amazing ancestral lines they derived from. This practice, in ancient Greece, was an offshoot of ancestral worship but, eventually evolved beyond those who shared a blood relation into the national sphere.

It was commonly considered that the heroes of old were the mixed offspring of immortals and mortals, or gods and the daughters of men. This mixed genealogy gave them powers and geniuses that we would consider to be superhuman. Interestingly, but not surprisingly, many of these heroes were tormented by higher powers, or gods, throughout their lives and this agony formed the plots for their mythical feats. The heroes of today are worshipped with excessive adulation in similar fashion. Many of today's idols/heroes are the athletes, cinematic celebrities, and music artist presented to the earth by the system of pop culture.

The concept of HRU/Horus existed before the heritage principle of the Greek hero/heroine. HRU (pronounced Huh-Roo), an ancient Egyptian Neteru, upheld the ethics of Ma'at (Balance, Truth, Reciprocity, Justice, Order, Harmony, and Propriety). HRU's name can be transliterated as "the light", "the one who is distant", "that which is above", or "upon". We see his story played out in so many works of art and film as he is the foundational script for the hero story. HRU is the young prince raised by his mother and absent father. In fact, HRU comes into being by way of an immaculate conception between his deceased father who, at the time, rules the underworld and his mother Isis/AUSET. He spent the larger part of his life battling his uncle, SET. SET was an agent of disorder while HRU's aim was to reinstate the order of Ma'at.

We cite these historic examples because it provides us with the basis for the surviving framework and paradigm referenced when we hear a call for a champion. These are the supernatural models that men are expected to endeavor towards. Despite the historical fact that many of these stories were hyperboles fabricated for the sole purpose of establishing a perspective of an ancestral era, that truly never existed. Those aspirant heroes, unaware of this reality, armed with nothing but human faculties would find themselves relentlessly shooting for the sun but, falling short among the clouds.

As Original people in North American, our assertions of our lives in antiquity can be over exaggerated in an attempt to counter the degradation experienced under the yolk of systemic racism. The indiscriminate claims of royal ancestry are a reaction to the African holocaust's nonstop offensive on the male and female ego. The extremities of the psychological operation of chattel slavery, and subsequent white supremacy/racism, motivate an equally extreme internal response. Throughout the years there have been many attempts to thwart the melanin dominant's efforts to recover their sense of self respect, dignity, lineage, language, religion, and self-definition. One of the longstanding devices has been to hold the despotic white male as the standard for achievement and, "normalcy", up to the women and children of the melanin dominant male. When the Negro man is unable to achieve that uniform target, the entire family unit harbors resentment towards him and he becomes disillusioned and disappointed in himself for not being able to attain what has been made to seem so obtainable, if only he would work hard enough for it. Eventually the same opportunities that have been misrepresent for him are tacitly offered to his female counterpart. Through legislative assistance, financial subsidies, and relaxed militaristic pressure she is able to obtain what he could not. In this way the negro female becomes the stated heroine of the melanin dominant people. The natural scales are imbalanced in this way and ultimately Negro male and female become angry and resentful towards one another for having to position in roles that neither one of them are truly designed for. This is how the original team is divided.

The division of the Black household weakens the power base of the Negro community. As Black is a consciousness, in context, we see that the guiding mind of the community is disrupted when natural roles are ignored, schemed upon, and distorted. There are examples of this familial warfare tactic dating back to the slave making plantations found in North America. In those times, the Negro female was given superior treatment on the human breeding farms whenever she would produce a new "sucker" (child). She was often given a gift or a coin for every child that she produced for the slave maker. The irony of this arrangement was that she was given coinage that she had no ability to travel anywhere and spend. She was able to stockpile a small store of coins, while her natural counterpart received nothing but, more labor to perform and the heartbreaking common experience of seeing his offspring taken to the auction block.

This premeditated wall built between Negro man and woman obscures the divine reflection each is naturally able to observe in one another. The film Hancock (2008) illustrates these points brilliantly. In the blockbuster movie Hancock, played by Will Smith, is a dysfunctional superhero who battles with alcoholism and indifference in reaction to emotional pain and loneliness. Despite Hancock's dysfunction he has a natural penchant to help others, despite often causing millions of dollars in damages as a result. Through the course of events in the picture we come to find out that Hancock has a sibling/wife by the name of Mary (Played by Charlize Theron), who has married herself to a human by the name of Ray Embrey (played by Jason Bateman). Mary's mating, with Ray, represents her joining herself with humankind. This happening was able to occur because Hancock is currently suffering from amnesia due to an attack that he suffered years earlier. When Mary found him in a hospital suffering from amnesia, with no history of her, she took it upon herself to abandon him after a three-thousand-year relationship. As a result of this disclosure Hancock comes to find out that he and Mary will remain immortal as long as they stay apart from each other. The moment they draw near to each other, they begin to become like humans and are no longer impervious to bodily harm. In the film Mary tells Hancock that when they are near to one another they lose their power to love, connect, grow, and eventually will die. Mary speaks about being hunted by "them" over the course of their chronological timeline but, does not cite who "they" are. We can surmise that "they" is an insinuation to the trappings of humanity and its sickened mental disposition that charges it to destroy what is different and unable to be effortlessly comprehended. The "they" is the overall energy of humanity that weakens them as Gods. The theme of the movie leaves the audience with the subtle warning that older, original, genetically superior individuals should not mate with one another because when they do, they lose all of the advantages that make them superior. As Hancock's character and Mary are siblings, this same ideology could be applied to any kinship that remains among divine beings. The concept that isolation, despite the depression and loneliness it fuels, is what is best for Original people is analogous to the incongruous practice of providing small coinage per baby to the enslaved Negro female.

From the historical disassociation tactics waged between melanin rich female and male animosity, resentment, anger, and distrust saturate the space between the two. Tragically, if one were to reach out to the other to restore the ruptured bond between them, that individual is likely to be met with trepidation or hostility. Though it has been officially legalized for the Negro man and woman to marry there are still binds placed on the emotional and mental anatomy of the two. The premise in the film Hancock, however insidious, has a sliver of truth. There is power that is lost when original man and woman come together to "know" one another, as in the biblical sense (Genesis 4:1). When a man ejaculates, he does release his power into the woman. When the woman gives birth, she does release a portion of her power into the child. This provides more dimension to the reason in naming Will Smiths character Hancock (masturbation) and Charlize Theron's character Mary (mother Mary). Regardless of such ideas, it is incumbent upon the modern-day Negro male and female coupling to create a standard for each other that reflects the authentic measure of heroism that is required of each of them. This enterprise will require a breaking down old walls of gender animosity and bitterness and the reconstruction of a paradigm of unconditional service to each other.

DROWNING

6

Life is unrehearsed. It's real time.

Focused direction is one of the elementary hallmarks of manhood. In order for men to take their natural positions as leaders of their homesteads and civic assemblies, they must have a clear internal vision of what the realization of their divine mission will develop to be. When the internal psychic pool is disquieted by so many diverse ideas, the way to clarity can be confounded by the profundity of choices. Who defines a what a man is? What defines what a man is to be? These questions can lead to many an adventure of disenchantment, discovery, and jubilation. Males are wired to learn in two primary ways, uniquely:

•Males learn via trial and error.

•Males learn from more advanced males who are further down the road than they are.

There are so many times when the male ego is affronted in Western society that seasoned men must maneuver, daily, an active minefield of political correctness, gender distortion, emotional guilting, and economic oppression. Without an unyielding sense of self shaping and determination it becomes increasingly demanding for a male to stand on the convictions of his cherished perspective. How does one begin to walk a tapered path when there are so many corridors presented to the multitudes of civilization which all claim to be the way to success, salvation, and wealth? In truth, many of these paths are the required roads that we must travel to arrive in the place that we must find ourselves. The only way out is to go through it, not over it.

There would appear to be a deliberate campaign to stir confusion within the masculine illustration of the divine among the Negro people. The Black male is provided a set of standards that he should aspire to but then destabilized at every turn, which produces a high level of hurt and frustration. Those models are alien to his spiritual, biological, psychological, cultural, political, sexual, and historical makeup. This reality becomes the dissonance constantly rising in the back of his head but, he is given no time to ponder on these things because he must hurry the process of "acting like a real man". When he sees no prototypes to appropriately express his hurt, then depression ensues. Where does he find the models which authenticate what he is feeling? The masculine journey of discovery and, even, emotional expression is external on display for the world to observe. When the models are befuddled there is no path to surrender to in order to train towards manhood.

In the position of total confusion with all odds against the Negro male, survival and achievement seem virtually impossible. The question on the table should intelligibly shift from what the clarification points of Black manhood are to what the disrupting standards of non-Black masculinity are. It is the universal grouping of males into categories based on personal perceptions of what manliness is that is considered to be what causes the greatest misperception. When manhood is defined by behavior, integrity, honorability, and community responsibility the vision begins to take form.

There is a driving compulsion that provides a sense of motivation in all young males towards the uncovering of their place in their community. Males, typically, want to leave their mark. In order for any man to institute a legacy the experience that unfolds for him should mirror his full right to expand and add onto what he experiences in life. The masculine principle is committed to the addition concept while the female idea is committed to the subtractive notion. When openings for expansion are denied to him, the male begins to invest in circular pursuits to vindicate manhood by movement, albeit cyclical. In the absence of forward motion durational activities such as purposeless baby-making, senseless violence, vanity, alcoholism, drug abuse, womanizing, and anything that ultimately consumes time with no productive outcome becomes the new measuring stick for machismo.

The motivation to arise in the dawning and apply yourself to a purpose is the anticipated future of all males. When the negro male is unsure of what the future holds, partly because he is a hunted species fighting just for mere survival, he loses the rightness of his pride of strength. He views his physique, sharp mind, and assertive will but, finds no place or need for them. His exquisitely bestowed gender gifts begin to atrophy and are finally viewed as the curse of his existence. Coupled with the lack of defining masculine influences, he finds himself crafting new representations of responsibility. His facility to respond with ability becomes how he defines manhood, for himself.

The rising man looks to redefine his connection with nature while birthing into realization what his mind has been able to conceive. The contrasting dissonance mentioned earlier begins to block his Innervisions. When masculine Innervisions are imprecise, then the feminine wisdom of what women should create is also vague. If he is unwilling to create his own definitions relating to what surrounds him, and how it all signifies the framework of his purpose, he will find himself drowning in a sea of possible directions while unable to create or produce.

In countless ancient cultures there is a tradition akin to the Aboriginal Walkabout or the First Nation Vision Quest. During these procedures a young man at the margins of obtaining manhood is sent into the wild, far away from his home community. He often is sent with nothing but, the clothes on his back and is required to inaugurate his own association with his spirit guides. Instinctive direction must be discovered while that young male is acting alone in the face of his guiding creator. These rite of passage experiences give the young male the confidence of communal acknowledgement because there is an outline provided for how the sacredness of manhood must initiate. This process will usually contain a ceremonial fast along with activities that are overseen by the community elders. The interpretation of dreams or metacognitive visions is encouraged. In some cultures, the young male is not permitted to return to the community until he receives his personal vision, spirit song, revelation of animal or astral guides, ancestral message, or life purpose. This activity happens in many arrangements but, usually occurs after the age of 12, and before the age of 15. The procedure is known to take anywhere from 3 days to 12 months, depending on the culture. In comparison to this ancient practice, consider the amount of time an adolescent male in western culture is given to reinforce, and verify, his spiritual, communal, and sexual comprehension. Often the adolescent Negro male, in the Anglosphere, is shielded from any true transformative experience that would instill a degree of mental freedom as uninhibited thinking is considered an act of war when demonstrated by the melanin dominant male.

The persistent insistence of critical thinking becomes the dire component in the personal compass of each, and every, Negro male. There is a baptismal of fire that the North American Negro male must undergo, whether by choice or social design. The preparation that assist the male to suitably face and answer the myriad of religious, sexual, spiritual, financial, cerebral, and chronological choices that he is predetermined to encounter must be centered on a communal rite of passage design. In this way his self-esteem is cultivated, and his proven abilities are corroborated by his onlooking community. This permits him to be encircled by the diversity of world thought, history, and culture but not be swayed away from the commencing vision provided to him by his Creator and Maker.

THIN LINE

7

When love is not reciprocated, more often than not a duality between love and hate emerges. A person who is loved can be loved and hated, concurrently, because of how they receive the love directed towards them by an individual. Often, we are unaware of our true measurement of "lovability". If we consider ourselves "good" or "lovable" then it is unfathomable that someone we may love could not return your love. With the warlike attack on the self-esteem and dignity of the melanin rich community, it is very easy to fall into a mesh of hate because of the blow it serves to one's ego and self-respect.

When the vulnerability of love is realized in the mind of a lover, there is gateway that is opened in the form of the proverbial heart. From the heart we see the outpouring of love or hate. In fact, the electric sensations of love or hate are manifested in the same areas of the body. There can be an addiction and longing for emotional food that radiates the pulsations of hate or love, as it does not matter to one who wants to receive a "fix" of that passionate stimulation in those particular areas.

—

Loving and engaging with each other based on novel definitions is in such jeopardy that even the phraseology we utilize to define our love derives from unfamiliar culture. The negro male is entangled in delineations that keep him in a script that weakens him and establishes idols in his psyche. This personal re-enslavement is a result of love being weaponized.

The male principle provides life and nurturing to the female principle. This dynamic often accounts for the continual need for attention that the female experiences. The hankering of attention is a calling for cultivation and the extension of life. The female principle should be portrayed with boldness and never used to pit itself against the male principle. When a Negro woman arrives in her full dignity there is a stance that emits from her essence. She comes with a need to connect with the other vital quintessence, which we know as man. The partnership between the original man and woman is motivated by the necessity to start a family. When they are viewing each other from new world definitions that transport only detrimental impressions of one another, they are unable to entwine themselves in their natural systematic manner. This becomes the peril in mating.

There is no mother principle without a father principle. The establishment of what we refer to as *"Black Love"* is founded in the nation building principle of family creation. The wholeness of a woman is determined by the connection she establishes with a man who is moving in corresponding direction. Wholeness is the vital key to utility. Throughout the globe Original people have been programmed to be productive material slaves. This can establish a new stumbling block within a relationship. If marriages and relationships are formed because of what our errant animal or material spirit agrees to, we soon grow uninterested and confused because of the separation between love, sex, and materialism (as dictated to us in the Western world).

The operating lifeblood of the female principle is a high imperative in the true development of the Negro child. The reality of the value of the female principle was so widely upheld in some cultures that during the first 3 years of breastfeeding the original child, male or female, there was no sexual intercourse between the father and mother. During this time the breast was given to the child to provide it a greater degree of security, social connectedness, and discipline. The recognized sacredness of the woman goes beyond her womb. This inviolability always extends to the way she guarded her body in performing the work that was needed to build a strong people in proper deportment to establish a strong nation.

The value system of how the Negro man and woman interact with one another begins with the emphasis on the spiritual element. There is a chi that pervades the string that interrelates all forces. Life on earth is understood by the study of our indigenous principles as this instructs us as to the primal instincts intrinsic in the male/female connection. The Anglosphere teaches us that all dilemmas are separate and disconnected. This is the exclusion of the spiritual principle. The indigenous value system of the Original coupling lets us know that all issues are connected, and the connection performs a part of a whole, as are all problems in society. If there is a corrupt society then it is a product of an ill-conceived social structure. There are no isolated incidents.

When melanin dominant male and female begin to see one another as enemies they frequently isolate thoughts without comprehending the fact that it is the social structure of white supremacy/racism which has taught them to hate one another. The cultural fundamentals that many Original people rely on has been stripped of its spiritual and historical values. It is from the viewpoint of determining the purpose of Black Love we begin to reposition our mapping along the "thin line" of love and hate. The Western society is not able to sustain the principle of marriage. With a 51% divorce rate and the remaining 49% containing couples who do not like one another, cheat on each other, or provide no life sustaining values towards each other it would only be an exercise in insanity to allow that segment of the world *think tank* to educate the Original couple on the significance of mating.

By means of the model of interconnectedness and oneness we can determine that what "I do for you, I do for myself" and "What I do to you, I do to myself". There is the indication of the spiritual thread that runs between the Negro male and female that ensure that that we see each other as a whole unit and not the necessary evils sitting on opposing lines of a divide. When we learn to feed into the call of ourselves as Original people and what the Creator has built into the Negro cooperative, we see our great reliance upon it. This restructuring of thought restructures the format of our relationships, and ultimately our entire worldview. The thought of unity that translates into the marital relationship between men and women gives a binding to the pair beyond sex. This needs to be witnessed by the determinedly Black adolescent. The young child begins to comprehend the personification of what a love story should be by their own terms.

When purpose is not given to a child, they see no value in their mate selection. As the Negro adolescent is trained for the world by their own Elders, they come forward with no need to prove femininity or masculinity to the world. They are robust and strengthened in their identity because they were mothered by the Original woman and trained for the global environment by the Original man. It is the jealousy of unfamiliar groups that cause them to study the strengths and weaknesses of the Original people. There must be vaster wisdom imputed into the Original couplings in order to avoid the pitfalls that many who they have been socially trained fall into.

Once the Negro male and female becomes wise to the truth that they are the product of a love story, they will begin to see how all things around them are connected. When they look at the historical chronicle, they appreciate why secret societies existed in ancient indigenous communities to prepare young males and young females for marriage. This is why arranged marriage had a such high success rate. The female and male were trained in their indispensable disciplines, respectively. This training deterred them from wasting time on dating games and sensuous experiences that would only lead into a later atomic explosion into the sacred temple of Black love.

There needs to be a prolongation of Black Love through the creation of children. The constant love between African man and African woman, with children, establishes the underlying theme of the esteem that the man and woman encase one another in. The bond between man and woman structures the matter of the family. To renew to a place of rulership the Original family must move beyond thwarted definitions given to them by the oppressive society they find themselves in. They must work towards uplifting the successful models of relationships that do not deaden African love or mobilize them towards bizarre sexual movements. There has to be an expansion towards scholarship with an indigenous Negro worldview that defends and discharges the attacks on original womanhood and manhood.

When a child comes forth inside of a community, the entire community must love that child as it is their own. The Negro male must surround himself by men who are living the reality of Black love and consider themselves responsible for his welfare. Despite what the external societies have thrown at the original coupling, they must struggle to not allow these attacks to turn them into monsters.

CONCLUSION

8

"Each of us is something of a schizophrenic personality, tragically divided against ourselves".

- Martin Luther King

This work only addresses a few of the inner demons that have been projected into the man of Blackness, known as the Black man. These misconceptions, that he has become a casualty of, have become his ailment. No longer can this information be suppressed. The idea that, at his rudiments, the Original man is maligned beyond the point of coupling, family managing, community leading, and loving are extraordinary delusions. The evidence of ancient cultures, long existing prior to European and Arab colonization, show an advanced and structured mind that existed within the Original male and female, as well as an affinity with the arch-energies that govern the universe. The Black male was never a Godless heathen but, rather established a culture that derived from his beautiful connection to the divine. That consecrated relationship established a balance across the earth's surface. Through his spiritual devotion he kept the globe healthy and the planet produced the right nutrients to keep his entire community resilient and empowered. After the introduction of extraneous societies who aimed to decimate these cultures, deplete them of their resources, and wage atrocities across the planet he began to lose his connective responsibility with the planet and his spiritual understanding began to dissolve. At that point he lost command of his place in the world.

The Negro male is caught in a cycle of self-loathing, impotency, and self-suppression of his greatest talents. His intellectual analysis of himself has been paralyzed because of the prevailing system which rules over his consciousness and keeps him in a place where he is perpetually defending himself from the ridicule hurled upon him by the perception of the masses. When the "NoirMale" is a victim of this psychic tyranny he begins to lose his capacity to govern himself and seeks out a hierarchal structure which will rule him. This complicit governorship now incapacitates his ability to explore and experience his own private destination of freedom.

In order to overthrow this position of power that lies above the awareness of the Negro male he must be able to identify the advents of his own false ego that have been manufactured by his desire to be ruled. Ironically, the Melanin-dominant male seeks to be ruled by those who have implanted the infection of this false impression of himself. The Negro male must realize that he is the fuel for the organism that keeps him at a disadvantage. He is the food of the beast which stalks him as prey and his ability to step away while stealing himself back into nature will begin to re-grow the underdeveloped male inside of him. To grow he must be willing to remove himself from his fear mongering overlords so, that he can develop outside of his flight or fight reactions. His energy must be allocated to his evolution and not to fending off the external attacks that seek to further disrupt his peace.

The Original man is toppling himself because he has allowed himself to become the caricature and urban myth that the fabricated ego would have him believe he is. This false sense of self even manufactures false threats that he feels he must be in persistent fear of. The ego is the false self. This statement already implies that the self is true, while the ego is false. The ego survives by way of offense and chronology. The wayward Negro male is a product of social ego and that personality eats from its host like any parasite would. The true self of the Original man is the host.

This is a delicate work that needs to be addressed among Original men, individually, and then collectively. The sickness that we allow to live within us, ultimately expresses itself outside of us. There should be no failure in seeing our dysfunction reflected out into the world by way of oppression, suppression, discrimination, racism, plagues, poverty, global catastrophes, failed marriages, unclaimed children, and so forth. Which of these conditions does not reflect that which is happening inside of the psyche of every Original male? To actuate operative change, even after countless attempts, the Negro male must face himself. Failing to take notice of what has been established inside of his own spirit and intellect, is the failure to improve himself, family, and community.

All of the truths that have been in this work should allow for the removal of these ideas long held about the Original man. Our personal demons are often the qualities that we have perceived in others and are an echo of the qualities within that we wish we could eliminate or amplify. As we pull these thoughts and ideas out into the open, we cease to take our pain and hatred out on the defenseless victims of our own inner confoundedness. We are unconsciously mutilating and torturing our own psyche like animals in a slaughterhouse or laboratory. Our psyche has been developed for the purpose of becoming a commodity for others. Come to know your hallowed darkness and reject the imposition of blasphemous darkness that seeks to live from your amazing contracting and expanding movement of evolution.

Let this sacred work be the catalyst for you to exorcise the hurt that has been positioned inside of you and the programming that has masqueraded itself as love in your lives. We will take ownership of ourselves, once again. This is a time that the equilibrium of power is beginning to turn on its head because the divine is bringing the hate-filled to justice. Let us first face our own interior demons, and then project that personal dignity for ourselves into the world.

NOIRMALE MUSIC
9

This literary work is the brother-work to a music expression, entitled "NoirMale", that provides insight and deeper meaning to all that has been written in this text. Please stream and share the "NoirMale" music EP on these popular music streaming platforms:

ABOUT THE AUTHOR
10

Follow me on all social media platforms **@ChiefYuya**

Go to ChiefYuya.com to subscribe to my podcast and get all upcoming news and events. I am the author of many more works on various subjects. Please visit my website ChiefYuya.com to explore more of my titles.

I also teach classes at the SaduluHouse.com on spirituality, self-development, and many more subjects to make sure you are the recipient of great information to grow in the right direction.

If you are interested in being a part of my Ministry movement, ANU Life Global Ministries, go to ANULIFEGLOBAL.org. We are an international ministry and are primarily service based.

Thank You!